Breaking The Fear Bubble

For Sales Engineers

Chris Fontaine

Breaking The Fear Bubble for Sales Engineers

Copyright © 2024 Chris Fontaine

All rights reserved.

ISBN: 9798303613966

Chris Fontaine

Breaking The Fear Bubble for Sales Engineers

- INTRODUCTION 7
- CHAPTER 1: FEAR AS THE FIRST OBSTACLE 13
- CHAPTER 2: PERCEPTION OVER PANIC 19
- CHAPTER 3: CONTROL THE CONTROLLABLES 25
- CHAPTER 4: ACTION IN THE FACE OF ADVERSITY . 33
- CHAPTER 5: EMOTIONAL DETACHMENT FROM OUTCOMES 41
- CHAPTER 6: FINDING STRENGTH IN CONSTRAINTS 49
- CHAPTER 7: LEARNING FROM REJECTION 57
- CHAPTER 8: COLLABORATION WITHOUT EGO 65
- CHAPTER 9: EXCELLENCE THROUGH SIMPLICITY 75
- CHAPTER 10: BECOMING THE CALM WITHIN THE CHAOS 83
- CHAPTER 11: THE ENDURANCE TO SUCCEED 91
- CHAPTER 12: THE LEGACY OF A SALES ENGINEER 99
- THE FEAR BUBBLE: A SALES ENGINEER'S CALL TO ACTION 107

Chris Fontaine

INTRODUCTION

There is a peculiar kind of fear that cloaks the world of Sales Engineering, a fear that remains unspoken yet palpable in every negotiation, every demo, and every pitch. It lingers in the awkward silence after a technical question you might not fully understand, in the split-second flicker of doubt before delivering an answer, and in the relentless pressure to transform curiosity into closed deals. To the untrained observer, Sales Engineers are paragons of confidence, technical fluency, and adaptability, but beneath that polished surface often lies a cauldron of apprehension, uncertainty, and self-doubt. This is the fear bubble, an invisible yet omnipresent force that shapes every interaction, decision, and outcome in the life of an SE.

This book is not a manual, nor is it a collection of easy hacks to "succeed in sales" by outsmarting your competition. Instead, it is a guide, a deeply personal and practical exploration of how we, as Sales Engineers, can break free from the grip of fear and reclaim our potential. Drawing on timeless principles of resilience, clarity, and courage, *Breaking the Fear Bubble* seeks to redefine how we approach the challenges of this unique profession. These ideas are not new, but their application to the nuanced world of Sales Engineering is revolutionary.

Fear is not unique to Sales Engineers, but our role amplifies it in ways few others experience. We straddle two worlds, the technical and the commercial, with expectations to master both. We are expected to understand a product's architecture inside and out while simultaneously crafting narratives that resonate with the client's business needs. We must be logical, adaptable, and deeply empathetic, often within the same meeting. This duality is our strength, but it is also our greatest challenge. And challenges, as history reminds us, are not to be avoided; they are to be confronted, understood, and transformed.

The philosopher Marcus Aurelius once wrote, "The impediment to action advances action. What stands in the way becomes the way." This principle underpins everything you will encounter in this book. The obstacles you face as a Sales Engineer, unrealistic deadlines, uncooperative clients, shifting goals, and even your own insecurities, are not merely roadblocks; they are the path itself. Through these challenges, you will find growth, resilience, and ultimately, success. But to walk this path requires a fundamental shift in perspective:

from viewing fear as an enemy to embracing it as a teacher.

In the chapters ahead, we will delve into the heart of Sales Engineering, dissecting the fears that hold us back and reimagining them as opportunities to grow. We will learn to see through the fog of uncertainty and develop clarity in moments of chaos. We will explore the power of taking consistent, deliberate action, even when outcomes are uncertain. And we will examine how humility, simplicity, and emotional detachment are not just virtues but essential tools for thriving in this demanding role.

This journey is not about becoming fearless. Fear is an integral part of the human experience, a signal that something important is at stake. Instead, this book is about breaking the bubble of fear that distorts our vision, paralyzes our decision-making, and erodes our confidence. It is about learning to move through fear with grace and purpose, armed with timeless tools and the unique strengths of a Sales Engineer.

If you've ever doubted yourself in a client meeting, hesitated to take a bold step for fear of rejection, or felt overwhelmed by the sheer complexity of your role, this book is for you. It is a call to action, a challenge to rethink how you approach obstacles, and an invitation to transform your relationship with fear. Because at its core, breaking the fear bubble isn't just about becoming a better Sales Engineer, it's about becoming a stronger, more resilient human being.

The obstacles are waiting. Let's transform them into opportunities.

Chris Fontaine

Chapter 1: Fear as the First Obstacle

Fear is the uninvited guest that arrives without warning and overstays its welcome. In Sales Engineering, it often shows up dressed as doubt, hesitation, or that gnawing feeling in the pit of your stomach right before a big presentation. This is the "fear bubble." It's not just a fleeting emotion; it's a state of mind that surrounds and isolates, whispering that you're not ready, not good enough, or that failure is inevitable. It feeds on uncertainty and magnifies every perceived weakness until it feels inescapable. But here's the truth: the fear bubble is an illusion, a transient moment that only has as much power as you allow it to hold.

To understand the fear bubble, you first have to acknowledge its existence. In Sales Engineering, fear manifests in many forms. It's the fear of rejection when a client doesn't respond to your carefully crafted demo. It's the fear of failure when a technical integration doesn't go as planned. It's the fear of falling short of quotas, of being judged by metrics that don't always capture the complexity of your role. These fears are not unique to Sales Engineers, but the nature of the job amplifies them. You're the bridge between technical possibilities and business realities, carrying the weight of expectations from both sides. It's a balancing act, and fear thrives in the tension.

Stoicism offers a lifeline in these moments. One of the core tenets of stoicism is the idea that we suffer more in imagination than in reality. Marcus Aurelius, the Roman emperor who moonlighted as a philosopher, once wrote, "If you are pained by external things, it is not they that disturb you, but your own judgment of them. And it is in your power to wipe out that judgment now." This is the essence of the fear bubble: it's a judgment, not a fact. Fear is your mind's way of projecting worst-case scenarios onto the blank canvas of the future. But the canvas is yours to paint.

Take a common scenario: You're about to present a complex solution to a room full of skeptical stakeholders. As you set up your slides, you notice your palms sweating and your heart racing. The fear bubble begins to form, filled with thoughts like, "What if I can't answer their questions?" or "What if they hate my solution?" But step back for a moment. What has actually happened? Nothing. The room is still quiet, your slides are still loaded, and you are still in control. The fear bubble exists only in your mind, fueled by possibilities that have yet to materialize.

Breaking the fear bubble requires a shift in perception. Start by recognizing fear for what it is: a signal, not a stop sign. Fear points to what matters most. If you're nervous about a demo, it's because you care about delivering value. If you're worried about rejection, it's because you believe in the potential of your solution. Reframing fear as an indicator of importance transforms it from an obstacle into a guide.

Another stoic strategy is to focus on what you can control. In any high-pressure situation, there are elements within your influence and others beyond it. You can't control whether a client's CFO suddenly decides to cut budgets mid-project, but you can control how prepared you are to address their concerns. You can't guarantee that a demo will go flawlessly, but you can ensure that you've tested it thoroughly and rehearsed potential responses to questions. By narrowing your focus to what is within your power, you deflate the fear bubble and reclaim your sense of agency.

Fear is also diminished through action. The fear bubble thrives in the space between intention and execution. It's in the pause before you pick up the phone to call a client, in the moments of hesitation before you click "Send" on a proposal. The longer you linger, the more the bubble grows. But the moment you act, the moment you take a step forward, fear loses its grip. Action disrupts the feedback loop of anxiety and replaces it with momentum.

As a Sales Engineer, you're no stranger to the iterative process. You tweak solutions, refine presentations, and adapt to feedback. Breaking the fear bubble follows the same principle. It's not about eliminating fear altogether, that's neither realistic nor desirable. Fear serves a purpose; it sharpens your focus and signals what's at stake. But like any tool, it must be used wisely. When you confront fear head-on, when you name it, question it, and act despite it, the bubble bursts. What's left is clarity, confidence, and the space to excel.

This transformation isn't linear. Some days, fear will feel manageable; other days, it will feel overwhelming. But each time you break through the fear bubble, you gain a deeper understanding of your capabilities. You learn that fear doesn't diminish your potential, it reveals it. It shows you where you need to grow, where you need to focus, and where you need to act.

In the end, fear is not the enemy. It's a companion on the journey, a reminder that you're stepping into the unknown and challenging yourself to grow. The fear bubble may form again and again, but each time you break it, you become stronger, more resilient, and more prepared for whatever lies ahead. And in the high-stakes, ever-evolving world of Sales Engineering, that's not just valuable, it's essential. Growth happens on the edge of discomfort, and the fear bubble is just the beginning of that edge.

Chapter 2: Perception Over Panic

Perception shapes reality, a truth that Sales Engineers come to know intimately. When you're entrenched in the high-stakes world of complex solutions, endless client demands, and shifting priorities, your perspective becomes your most powerful tool. Challenges, after all, are inevitable. What defines your success isn't the absence of obstacles but how you perceive and respond to them. It's a simple but profound idea: we see what we choose to focus on. And in that choice lies the power to transform panic into opportunity.

The art of reframing begins with awareness. Imagine a deal teetering on the brink of collapse. The client has raised last-minute concerns, stakeholders are divided, and the clock is ticking. It's easy to fall into a spiral of frustration, seeing the situation as a crisis beyond repair. But what if, instead of viewing it as a disaster, you reframed it as a chance to deepen your understanding of the client's needs? What if you saw it as an opportunity to demonstrate adaptability, problem-solving, and grace under pressure? The situation itself hasn't changed, but your perception has. And with that shift comes the clarity to act.

Case studies abound of Sales Engineers who turned seemingly insurmountable challenges into defining successes. Take, for instance, a team pitching a cybersecurity solution to a client in the financial sector. Midway through the engagement, the client's priorities shifted due to a sudden regulatory update. What began as a straightforward proposal became a labyrinth of new requirements, tighter deadlines, and heightened scrutiny. The initial reaction?

Panic. But one Sales Engineer on the team paused and reassessed. They recognized the new requirements as an opportunity to highlight the solution's flexibility and scalability, tailoring the demo to address the updated needs explicitly. Their ability to reframe the challenge not only saved the deal but positioned the solution as indispensable to the client's compliance strategy.

This kind of success isn't accidental. It's the result of deliberate techniques that allow Sales Engineers to pause, assess, and respond with composure. The first technique is mastering the pause. In high-pressure situations, the instinct is often to act immediately, to fix things as quickly as possible. But action without thought often exacerbates the problem. The pause is a moment to gather information, regulate emotions, and plan your approach. It's not inaction; it's intentionality. Pausing allows you to respond rather than react.

The second technique is questioning your assumptions. Under stress, it's easy to fall into rigid thinking, seeing only the problem and not the possibilities. By asking open-ended questions, "What is the client truly concerned about?" "What solutions haven't we considered?" "How can I turn this into an advantage?", you shift your focus from obstacles to opportunities. This mindset not only helps you find solutions but also positions you as a trusted advisor who sees the bigger picture.

Finally, there's the power of visualization. Before stepping into a challenging meeting or presentation, take a moment to envision success. Imagine the client nodding in agreement, the stakeholders aligning behind your proposal, the solution being embraced with enthusiasm. This isn't wishful thinking; it's mental preparation. Visualization primes your mind for positive outcomes, boosting confidence and reinforcing your ability to navigate challenges effectively.

One of the most valuable lessons for Sales Engineers is understanding that perception is contagious. Your ability to remain calm, focused, and solutions-oriented influences everyone around you. Clients take their cues from your demeanor. Teams look to you for guidance. When you choose to see challenges as opportunities, you inspire others to do the same. It's a ripple effect that can turn the tide of even the most difficult engagements.

Perception over panic doesn't mean ignoring risks or sugarcoating difficulties. It's about acknowledging the reality of the situation while choosing to focus on what can be done rather than what can't. It's about shifting the narrative from "This is a problem" to "This is an opportunity to grow, to adapt, and to excel." And in a profession as dynamic and demanding as Sales Engineering, that perspective is not just helpful, it's transformative.

In the end, the way you perceive challenges determines the trajectory of your career. Panic leads to paralysis; perception leads to progress. By cultivating the ability to reframe, pause, and act with clarity, you not only navigate challenges more effectively but also set the stage for lasting success. The choice is yours: Will you see the obstacle or the opportunity? In that choice lies your greatest power.

Chapter 3: Control the Controllables

In Sales Engineering, control is a precious commodity, and an elusive one. The dynamics of the role are inherently unpredictable: shifting client needs, evolving technologies, and the ever-present specter of competition. Yet amidst this whirlwind, there lies a powerful truth borrowed from stoicism: focus only on what is within your control. By mastering this principle, Sales Engineers can navigate complexity with clarity, reduce unnecessary stress, and channel their energy where it truly matters.

The stoic philosopher Epictetus famously wrote, "Some things are up to us, and some things are not." This distinction is the cornerstone of controlling the controllables. While you can't dictate how a client's CFO will respond to your proposal, you can control the thoroughness of your preparation. You can't prevent a competitor from offering a lower price, but you can control how effectively you communicate your solution's unique value. This shift in focus, from external outcomes to internal efforts, is transformative. It reframes success not as a result of external validation but as a product of deliberate and intentional actions.

Let's start with the pre-sales process, where uncertainty often looms large. Imagine being tasked with delivering a proposal for a large enterprise client. The stakes are high, and the variables are many: diverse stakeholders with differing priorities, a complex decision-making process, and potential curveballs from competitors. It's easy to feel overwhelmed. But by focusing on what you can control, you create a roadmap through the chaos. This means ensuring your proposal is meticulously tailored to the client's needs, anticipating questions and objections, and preparing a clear narrative that connects your solution to their goals. These are within your power, and they're what ultimately influence the client's perception.

The same principle applies to technical demonstrations, those high-pressure moments where all eyes are on you to deliver. A demo can feel like a performance, with the pressure to impress hanging heavy in the air. But the reality is, not every aspect of a demo is within your control. A glitch might occur, or a stakeholder might fixate on a minor detail. What you can control is how prepared you are to handle these moments. Have you tested the demo under multiple conditions? Do you have backup plans in case of technical issues? Are you ready to pivot the conversation if the audience's focus shifts? By concentrating on these controllables, you not only reduce the likelihood of failure but also build the confidence to adapt in real time.

One of the greatest challenges Sales Engineers face is managing client concerns, many of which are outside their immediate sphere of influence. A client might hesitate to move forward due to budget constraints, internal politics, or competing priorities. While these factors are beyond your control, your response to them is not. By listening empathetically, asking thoughtful questions, and addressing the root of their concerns, you demonstrate a commitment to their success that transcends the immediate challenge. You can't always resolve their concerns, but you can control how you show up in those moments, as a trusted partner rather than a desperate vendor.

Focusing on what you can control also means embracing uncertainty without overcommitting to the outcome. Sales Engineers often grapple with the temptation to overpromise, driven by the desire to secure a deal or meet expectations. But overcommitting creates risks that can undermine trust and strain delivery teams. Instead, focus on controlling the clarity and honesty of your communication. Be transparent about what your solution can and cannot do, and emphasize your willingness to collaborate on finding the best path forward. This approach not only builds credibility but also positions you as a reliable and thoughtful problem-solver.

Strategies for controlling the controllables extend beyond individual engagements to your broader mindset. The first strategy is preparation. Preparation is your armor against the unknown. Whether it's researching a client's industry, rehearsing your presentation, or gathering insights from past engagements, preparation equips you to navigate uncertainty with confidence. It doesn't eliminate surprises, but it ensures you're ready to handle them.

The second strategy is prioritization. In a role as multifaceted as Sales Engineering, not everything can or should demand your attention. By identifying the areas where your efforts will have the greatest impact, you conserve energy and focus on what truly matters. This might mean focusing on high-value opportunities, addressing key client concerns, or refining the aspects of a solution that directly align with the client's goals.

The third strategy is adaptability. Even the best-laid plans can go awry, and resilience lies in your ability to pivot gracefully. Adaptability is not about abandoning your approach but about recalibrating it in response to new information. This might mean adjusting your demo on the fly to address an unexpected question or revising your proposal to align with updated client priorities. Adaptability ensures that you remain effective even when circumstances change.

Finally, controlling the controllables requires a commitment to continuous reflection. After every engagement, take the time to assess what worked, what didn't, and what you can improve. Reflection turns experience into insight, allowing you to refine your approach and grow with each challenge. It's a practice that not only enhances your performance but also reinforces your sense of agency and purpose.

In the ever-changing landscape of Sales Engineering, the ability to control the controllables is a superpower. It shifts your focus from the noise of external pressures to the clarity of intentional action. It empowers you to navigate uncertainty with confidence, adaptability, and grace. And most importantly, it reminds you that success is not about eliminating challenges but about mastering the art of responding to them. When you control the controllables, you don't just survive the chaos, you thrive within it.

Chapter 4: Action in the Face of Adversity

Action is the antidote to fear and the pathway to resilience. In Sales Engineering, where complex challenges and high stakes are the norm, hesitation can be costly. The ability to act decisively and consistently, even in the face of adversity, separates those who merely manage from those who thrive. This chapter is about embracing action as a tool to dissolve fear, build resilience, and turn obstacles into opportunities.

"Only action dissolves fear." It's a simple yet profound truth. When faced with uncertainty, whether it's a difficult client, a technical glitch, or a looming deadline, the mind often conjures worst-case scenarios. Left unchecked, these fears can paralyze decision-making, creating a cycle of inaction. But the moment you take a step forward, however small, the grip of fear begins to loosen. Action shifts your focus from what might happen to what you can do. It transforms uncertainty into momentum and creates the conditions for progress.

Practical action in Sales Engineering begins with preparation. Preparation is not just about gathering information; it's about equipping yourself to navigate complexity with confidence. Imagine yourself as the Sales Engineer, working on a high-profile deal with a global retailer. The client's requirements were extensive, their expectations high, and their timeline tight. Rather than succumbing to the pressure, the Engineer broke the challenge into manageable steps.

They conducted thorough research on the client's industry, anticipated potential objections, and rehearsed their presentation until it felt second nature. When unexpected questions arose during the pitch, they were ready, not because they knew every answer but because they had practiced staying composed under pressure. Their preparation laid the groundwork for decisive action, turning a daunting challenge into a career-defining success.

Action also requires resilience, the ability to persist through setbacks and adapt to changing circumstances. Resilience is built not in moments of ease but in the crucible of adversity. Take, for example, a Sales Engineer who faced repeated rejection from a prospect in the healthcare sector. Despite multiple no's, they refused to give up. Instead, they sought to understand the root of the prospect's resistance, asking thoughtful questions and offering tailored solutions. Over time, their persistence paid off. The prospect became not only a client but also a vocal advocate for the Engineer's solution. This success wasn't about a single grand gesture; it was the result of consistent, deliberate action that demonstrated commitment and value.

Another cornerstone of effective action is technical knowledge. In Sales Engineering, credibility is currency, and technical expertise is what earns it. When faced with adversity, a challenging question during a demo, a skeptical stakeholder, or a complex integration issue, your knowledge becomes your foundation. But technical knowledge alone is not enough; it must be paired with the ability to communicate effectively and adapt to the audience. The best Sales Engineers are not just technical experts; they are translators who bridge the gap between complex solutions and business value. This combination of expertise and communication empowers action, allowing you to navigate challenges with authority and clarity.

Success stories often highlight the transformative power of action. One such story involves a Sales Engineer who was tasked with turning around a failing project for a major financial institution. The initial rollout had been plagued by miscommunications and unmet expectations, leaving the client frustrated and disengaged. Rather than deflecting blame or retreating into damage control, the Engineer took ownership of the situation. They organized a series of workshops with the client's team to identify pain points, recalibrate the solution, and rebuild trust. These workshops not only resolved the immediate issues but also uncovered new opportunities for collaboration. By taking decisive action, the Engineer transformed a potential failure into a long-term partnership.

Action in the face of adversity also means knowing when to pivot. Not every strategy will succeed, and clinging to a failing approach can compound the problem. The ability to recognize when a course correction is needed, and to act on it, is a hallmark of effective Sales Engineering.

This might mean revising your proposal to align with updated client priorities, shifting your demo to address unexpected questions, or seeking input from colleagues to gain new perspectives. Pivoting is not a sign of weakness; it's a sign of adaptability and strategic thinking.

Finally, action is about mindset. It's about embracing challenges as opportunities to grow, to learn, and to demonstrate value. Adversity is not a detour; it's part of the journey. By approaching each obstacle with curiosity and determination, you reframe it from a roadblock into a stepping stone. This mindset not only fuels action but also inspires those around you, creating a ripple effect of positivity and progress.

In the high-pressure, high-stakes world of Sales Engineering, action is not just a response to adversity; it is a strategy for success. By taking deliberate, consistent steps forward, you dissolve fear, build resilience, and create opportunities where others see only obstacles. The challenges you face are not barriers; they are invitations to excel.

And with every action you take, you move closer to mastery, proving that even in the face of adversity, progress is always possible.

Chapter 5: Emotional Detachment from Outcomes

Emotional detachment from outcomes is a skill most Sales Engineers learn the hard way. It's not about apathy or indifference, quite the opposite. It's about caring deeply while maintaining the emotional resilience to accept that, sometimes, things won't go your way. The stakes in Sales Engineering are high: deals that can make or break a quarter, presentations where every word feels like it's being scrutinized, and relationships that take months to nurture but can unravel in minutes. Yet the key to long-term success lies not in clinging to outcomes but in mastering the art of detachment.

Setbacks are inevitable. No matter how prepared you are, no matter how well you execute, there will be times when things don't work out. A critical stakeholder might veto your proposal. A demo might crash at the worst possible moment. A competitor might undercut your pricing. These moments can feel devastating if you tie your sense of self-worth to the outcome. But when you learn to detach, you see these setbacks for what they are: temporary and external. They are not reflections of your value or ability, but challenges to navigate and learn from.

Detachment doesn't mean disengagement. In fact, it's about balancing passion for your role with the perspective needed to weather disappointments. Imagine pouring weeks of effort into a proposal, only to have the client choose a different vendor. The initial sting is real, and it's natural to feel it. But dwelling on the loss doesn't change the outcome. Instead, detachment allows you to shift focus: What did I learn from this experience? How can I apply that learning to future opportunities? It's about moving forward without the emotional baggage that can cloud judgment and drain energy.

Stoicism offers profound insights into this practice. One of its core principles is understanding the difference between what is within your control and what is not. As a Sales Engineer, you control your preparation, your communication, and your effort. You do not control the client's budget, internal politics, or decision-making timeline. By focusing on what you can influence and accepting what you cannot, you free yourself from the frustration of trying to control the uncontrollable. The stoic philosopher Marcus Aurelius captured this beautifully: "You have power over your mind, not outside events. Realize this, and you will find strength."

Emotional resilience is a byproduct of detachment. When you're not fixated on outcomes, you're better equipped to handle the ups and downs of the role. Resilience allows you to approach challenges with clarity and composure, rather than being overwhelmed by frustration or disappointment. It creates space for thoughtful reflection and proactive problem-solving, ensuring that setbacks don't derail your progress.

Immerse yourself in the story of a Sales Engineer working with a major client in the manufacturing sector. After months of negotiations and multiple rounds of revisions, the client decided to delay the project indefinitely. The Engineer could have taken this as a personal failure, spiraling into self-doubt. Instead, they took a step back and reassessed. They reached out to the client to understand the reasons behind the delay, identifying internal resource constraints as the primary issue. Armed with this insight, they offered to provide interim support, maintaining the relationship and positioning themselves for future opportunities. Their ability to detach emotionally from the immediate outcome enabled them to see the bigger picture and keep the door open for collaboration.

Burnout is a significant risk in high-pressure sales roles, and detachment is one of the most effective safeguards against it. When you're emotionally invested in every outcome, the constant highs and lows can take a toll. Detachment doesn't mean you stop caring; it means you care strategically. You invest your energy in actions and decisions, not in worrying about results. This shift reduces stress and helps you sustain the passion and drive needed for long-term success.

Detachment also fosters better decision-making. When you're overly attached to a specific outcome, it's easy to make decisions driven by fear or desperation. You might overpromise to secure a deal or avoid addressing a critical issue to keep the client happy. Detachment allows you to approach situations objectively, prioritizing integrity and long-term value over short-term gains. It's a mindset that clients and colleagues respect, as it reflects confidence and professionalism.

Learning to detach is not easy. It requires self-awareness, discipline, and practice. Start by recognizing when your emotions are tied too closely to an outcome. Ask yourself: Am I focusing on what I can control, or am I worrying about factors beyond my influence? When setbacks occur, give yourself permission to feel the disappointment, but set a time limit. Acknowledge the emotion, then shift your focus to the lessons learned and the actions you can take moving forward.

Mindfulness practices can also support detachment. Techniques like deep breathing, meditation, or journaling help you stay grounded and present, reducing the emotional intensity of setbacks. These practices create a buffer between your emotions and your reactions, enabling you to respond thoughtfully rather than impulsively.

In the end, emotional detachment from outcomes is not about caring less; it's about caring wisely. It's about balancing passion with perspective, effort with acceptance. Detachment allows you to navigate the highs and lows of Sales Engineering with resilience and grace, maintaining your focus on what truly matters. And in a field as demanding and dynamic as this one, that balance is not just a skill, it's a superpower.

Chapter 6: Finding Strength in Constraints

Constraints are often seen as barriers, the proverbial immovable object standing in the way of progress. But for Sales Engineers, constraints are not the enemy; they are the canvas upon which ingenuity and creativity are painted. Whether it's a limited budget, a tight deadline, or a difficult client, what stands in the way becomes the way. Learning to embrace and leverage constraints isn't just a survival skill, it's a pathway to excellence.

The stoic principle that "what stands in the way becomes the way" speaks directly to the heart of this chapter. Challenges and limitations are not roadblocks; they are opportunities to refine processes, spark innovation, and push boundaries. This mindset doesn't come naturally to most. When faced with constraints, the default reaction is often frustration or defeat. But Sales Engineers who learn to pivot, adapt, and thrive under pressure discover that constraints can fuel some of their greatest successes.

Take the story of a Sales Engineer tasked with delivering a complex solution to a midsize company with a razor-thin IT budget. The client's needs were clear, but their financial limitations seemed insurmountable. Instead of walking away, the Engineer reframed the challenge. They worked closely with the client to identify essential features, streamline the scope of the solution, and find creative ways to integrate existing resources. The result? A tailored implementation that met the client's needs without exceeding their budget. The Engineer's ability to turn a financial constraint into a collaborative opportunity not only secured the deal but also strengthened the client relationship.

Resource limitations are not the only constraints Sales Engineers face. Time constraints are equally challenging. Imagine preparing for a high-stakes client demo with just 48 hours to customize the presentation. Every minute counts, and the margin for error is nonexistent. In such situations, prioritization becomes your superpower. By focusing on the most impactful elements of the demo and eliminating non-essential details, you can deliver a presentation that resonates despite the limited prep time. This approach requires discipline and clarity, but it also underscores the power of constraints to sharpen focus and drive results.

Difficult clients represent another form of constraint, one that tests your patience, adaptability, and emotional resilience. These are the clients who challenge every feature, question every price point, and seem impossible to please. Yet, they are also the clients who force you to elevate your game. Difficult clients demand deeper preparation, sharper communication, and a level of empathy that turns resistance into rapport. When handled effectively, these relationships often yield some of the most rewarding outcomes. By embracing their challenges, you not only meet their expectations but often exceed them, creating advocates out of adversaries.

Constraints also play a crucial role in fostering ingenuity. Limitations compel you to think differently, to approach problems from unconventional angles, and to find solutions that might otherwise remain undiscovered. In Sales Engineering, this might mean designing a solution that leverages open-source tools to cut costs or finding creative ways to demonstrate ROI for a skeptical client. Ingenuity thrives in the space where conventional options fall short. Constraints, rather than stifling creativity, often become the spark that ignites it.

The role of processes cannot be overlooked when dealing with constraints. Efficient, well-defined processes provide the structure needed to navigate limitations effectively. Whether it's a streamlined workflow for customizing demos or a checklist for addressing common objections, strong processes reduce the cognitive load and free you to focus on strategic thinking. They turn constraints from chaos into manageable challenges, ensuring that you stay proactive rather than reactive.

Constraints also teach humility and collaboration. When you can't solve a problem alone, you're forced to seek input from colleagues, clients, or cross-functional teams. This collaborative approach not only generates fresh ideas but also strengthens relationships. Constraints remind us that success in Sales Engineering is rarely a solo endeavor. It's built on the collective wisdom, effort, and creativity of everyone involved.

One of the most powerful lessons of working within constraints is the realization that perfection is not the goal. Clients don't expect perfection; they expect solutions that work. Constraints push you to prioritize what truly matters, to focus on delivering value rather than chasing unattainable ideals. This shift in mindset not only reduces stress but also aligns your efforts with the client's real needs, creating solutions that are practical, effective, and appreciated.

Finally, constraints cultivate resilience. Each time you navigate a limitation successfully, you build confidence in your ability to handle future challenges. Over time, constraints become less intimidating and more like familiar puzzles waiting to be solved. This resilience not only enhances your performance but also inspires trust in clients and colleagues alike. They see in you someone who doesn't shy away from challenges but embraces them with determination and ingenuity.

In the dynamic world of Sales Engineering, constraints are inevitable. But they are also invaluable. They force you to innovate, to adapt, and to grow. They reveal strengths you didn't know you had and push you to achieve outcomes you didn't think possible. When you learn to find strength in constraints, you unlock a level of creativity, collaboration, and resilience that sets you apart. Because what stands in the way doesn't just block the path, it becomes the path.

Chapter 7: Learning from Rejection

Rejection is a universal experience, yet it remains one of the most difficult to navigate. For Sales Engineers, rejection often feels personal, a reflection of effort seemingly dismissed, strategies questioned, or abilities doubted. But what if rejection wasn't an enemy to be avoided, but a mentor to be embraced? What if every "no" was an invitation to refine, adapt, and grow?

Rejection as a mentor requires a fundamental shift in mindset. It begins with recognizing that rejection is not the end of a process; it's an inflection point. In the high-stakes world of Sales Engineering, rejection is inevitable. Whether it's a deal that doesn't close, a demo that doesn't land, or a client who chooses a competitor, setbacks are part of the journey. What matters is how you respond. Do you dwell on the loss, or do you mine it for insights that will shape your next success?

Put yourself in the shoes of a Sales Engineer who spent weeks crafting a proposal for a leading technology firm. Every detail had been tailored, every angle considered, yet the client ultimately decided to go in another direction. Initially, the rejection stung. But rather than closing the chapter, the Engineer reached out to the client, not to challenge the decision, but to understand it.

Through honest and open feedback, they learned that while the solution had been technically sound, it lacked clarity in articulating ROI to non-technical stakeholders. Armed with this insight, the Engineer refined their messaging for future engagements, turning a setback into a stepping stone.

This process of learning from rejection is a cornerstone of stoic philosophy. Marcus Aurelius advised, "You have power over your mind – not outside events. Realize this, and you will find strength." Applied to Sales Engineering, this principle underscores the importance of focusing on what you can control: your preparation, your messaging, your adaptability. You cannot control a client's decision, but you can control how you prepare for and respond to it.

One of the most practical ways to leverage rejection is through the refinement of technical demonstrations. A failed demo can feel like a disaster in the moment, but it's also a goldmine of data. What questions stumped the audience? Where did engagement falter? What assumptions didn't hold up? By reviewing these moments with an objective eye, you can identify opportunities to improve. Maybe it's a matter of simplifying explanations, aligning features more closely with business objectives, or preempting common objections. Every demo, successful or not, is an opportunity to iterate and grow.

Adaptability is another critical lesson rejection teaches. No two clients are the same, and what resonates with one may alienate another. A Sales Engineer who treats every engagement as a template risks missing the nuances that drive client decisions. Rejection often highlights these blind spots. Maybe a client's priorities shifted mid-process, or maybe their concerns weren't adequately addressed. By approaching rejection with curiosity rather than defensiveness, you position yourself to adapt more effectively in the future.

Rejection also fosters resilience, the ability to persist in the face of setbacks. Each rejection is an opportunity to practice resilience, to reaffirm your commitment to growth, and to demonstrate that your value as a Sales Engineer isn't tied to any single outcome. Resilience isn't about ignoring rejection; it's about integrating it into your journey. It's about acknowledging the disappointment, learning from it, and moving forward with renewed determination.

The key to resilience is perspective. Ponder the Sales Engineer who repeatedly loses deals to a competitor offering a lower price. Instead of fixating on the frustration of the loss, they analyze the competitor's approach and identify gaps in their own strategy. Over time, they refine their messaging to emphasize the long-term value of their solution, making price a secondary consideration. This iterative process transforms rejection into a learning cycle, where each loss brings them closer to their next win.

A stoic approach to rejection also helps avoid the emotional traps that can accompany setbacks. It's easy to internalize rejection, to see it as a reflection of personal failure. But stoicism reminds us that external events are not inherently good or bad; it is our interpretation that gives them weight. By detaching your sense of self-worth from the outcome, you free yourself to focus on continuous improvement rather than self-criticism.

Some of the most successful Sales Engineers credit their greatest breakthroughs to moments of rejection. A failed pitch might lead to the discovery of a previously overlooked client need. A lost deal might inspire a new way to communicate value. Rejection, when approached with the right mindset, becomes a catalyst for innovation and growth.

Rejection also teaches humility. No matter how experienced or skilled you are, there will always be variables beyond your control. Humility allows you to accept these realities without letting them diminish your confidence. It's a reminder that success is not a straight line but a series of adjustments, recalibrations, and recoveries.

Ultimately, rejection is not a detour; it's part of the path. It's a mentor that teaches humility, adaptability, and resilience. By embracing rejection, Sales Engineers not only refine their craft but also strengthen their ability to navigate the complexities of the role. Rejection is not the end of the story; it's the beginning of a new chapter, one written with greater clarity, insight, and purpose.

Chapter 8: Collaboration Without Ego

Collaboration is the lifeblood of Sales Engineering, but true collaboration requires a key ingredient that many overlook: humility. It's easy to approach teamwork and client relations with the subconscious desire to prove yourself, to be the smartest person in the room, or to take ownership of the solution. But ego, unchecked, is a barrier, it clouds judgment, alienates stakeholders, and undermines trust. The best Sales Engineers know that letting go of ego isn't a sacrifice; it's a strategy for success. Collaboration without ego fosters creativity, strengthens relationships, and leads to better outcomes for everyone involved.

The role of humility in collaboration starts with acknowledging that you don't have all the answers, and you don't need to. Sales Engineering is a team sport, involving salespeople, technical experts, product teams, and clients. Each brings unique insights and expertise to the table. When you approach collaboration with humility, you create space for others to contribute, enriching the conversation and the solution. Humility doesn't diminish your authority; it enhances it by showing that you value the collective wisdom of the group.

Imagine a Sales Engineer working with a team to deliver a complex proposal for a multinational client. The Engineer has deep technical expertise and a clear vision for the solution. But during a brainstorming session, a junior team member suggests an unconventional approach that initially seems out of scope. Instead of dismissing the idea, the Engineer listens, asks questions, and explores its potential. The result? A hybrid solution that not only addresses the client's needs but also exceeds their expectations. By letting go of ego and embracing collaboration, the Engineer unlocked a level of creativity that wouldn't have been possible alone.

Ego also manifests in client relationships, often in subtle ways. It's the impulse to dominate a presentation, to showcase your expertise without fully listening to the client's concerns, or to push a preferred solution without considering alternative perspectives. But clients don't want a hero; they want a partner. Collaboration without ego means prioritizing the client's needs above your desire to impress. It means asking thoughtful questions, listening actively, and being willing to adapt your approach based on their feedback. This humility builds trust, demonstrating that you're not just there to sell a product but to solve a problem together.

The power of letting go of ego becomes even more evident in high-pressure situations. Imagine a scenario where a demo encounters unexpected technical issues. The Sales Engineer's ego might tempt them to deflect blame, to insist that the issue isn't significant, or to bulldoze through without addressing the audience's concerns. But humility takes a different approach. It acknowledges the issue openly, takes responsibility where appropriate, and invites collaboration to address it. This response not only diffuses tension but also reinforces credibility. Clients and colleagues value honesty and authenticity far more than an illusion of perfection.

Authenticity is a cornerstone of collaboration without ego. It's about showing up as your genuine self, free from the need to posture or compete. Authenticity creates an environment where others feel safe to share their ideas, voice their concerns, and contribute fully. It fosters a sense of psychological safety, where the focus shifts from individual performance to collective success. In a competitive field like Sales Engineering, authenticity is often the differentiator that sets great collaborators apart.

Building trust through authenticity also means being transparent about limitations. No solution is perfect, and no professional is infallible. When you're honest about what your product can and cannot do, you establish a foundation of trust that clients and colleagues can rely on. This transparency doesn't weaken your position; it strengthens it by showing that you're focused on finding the best path forward, not on protecting your ego.

Collaboration without ego is particularly vital in competitive environments. Sales Engineering often involves navigating conflicting interests, whether it's balancing the priorities of internal teams or addressing competing client demands. Ego thrives on conflict, turning disagreements into power struggles. Humility, on the other hand, seeks alignment. It focuses on understanding different perspectives, finding common ground, and working toward solutions that benefit everyone. This approach not only resolves conflicts more effectively but also strengthens relationships in the process.

One of the greatest advantages of collaboration without ego is its impact on problem-solving. Ego narrows focus, fixating on defending ideas or proving points. Humility broadens focus, opening the door to diverse perspectives and creative solutions. A Sales Engineer who approaches challenges with humility is more likely to uncover innovative approaches, leveraging the collective intelligence of the team. This adaptability is crucial in a field where no two problems are exactly alike.

Humility also enhances resilience. When you're not tied to being right or taking credit, setbacks feel less personal. Instead of dwelling on what went wrong, you can focus on what can be learned and improved. This resilience not only benefits your own growth but also inspires confidence in clients and colleagues, who see you as a steady, reliable partner even in challenging circumstances.

In the end, collaboration without ego is about shifting the focus from self to service. It's about recognizing that the best outcomes are rarely the result of individual brilliance but of collective effort. It's about building relationships rooted in trust, authenticity, and mutual respect. And it's about embracing humility not as a weakness, but as a strength that unlocks the full potential of collaboration.

Sales Engineers who master the art of collaboration without ego don't just deliver better solutions; they elevate everyone around them. They create environments where ideas flourish, relationships thrive, and challenges are met with creativity and resolve. By letting go of ego, they gain something far greater: the trust, respect, and loyalty of those they work with. And in a profession built on partnership and problem-solving, that is the ultimate measure of success.

Chris Fontaine

Chapter 9: Excellence Through Simplicity

Simplicity is a concept often underestimated in the complex world of Sales Engineering. With layers of technical jargon, intricate client demands, and competitive pressure, the default tendency is to overcomplicate. But simplicity is not about stripping away detail; it's about distilling the essence of a solution to make it clear, elegant, and impactful. Excellence, as it turns out, is often found in simplicity.

The stoic principle of minimalism offers a guiding philosophy: less is more. In the context of Sales Engineering, this doesn't mean doing less; it means doing what matters most. It means cutting through the noise to focus on delivering value. Marcus Aurelius once wrote, "If you seek tranquility, do less. Or more accurately, do what's essential." The same principle applies to crafting technical solutions and client communications, prioritize what is essential, and let go of the rest.

Place yourself in a scenario where a Sales Engineer is presenting a cybersecurity solution to a mid-sized healthcare organization. The product has dozens of features, each with its own technical merit. It's tempting to showcase everything, to prove the robustness of the offering. But the client doesn't need a tour of the entire toolbox; they need to know how the solution addresses their specific challenges. By focusing on the three features most relevant to the client's pain points and explaining them in simple, relatable terms, the Sales Engineer demonstrates mastery. Simplicity, in this case, is not a lack of detail but a clarity of focus.

The power of simplicity becomes even more apparent in client communication. Technical jargon, while familiar and comforting to experts, can alienate non-technical stakeholders. These stakeholders are often the decision-makers, and their understanding of a solution's value is key to closing a deal. Simplicity in communication means translating complex ideas into language that resonates with the audience. It's the difference between saying, "Our product leverages advanced machine learning algorithms to detect anomalies in real-time" and saying, "Our solution spots unusual activity immediately, helping you stop threats before they cause harm." Both statements convey the same idea, but the latter connects more directly to the client's priorities.

Simplicity also plays a crucial role in problem-solving. In the heat of a technical challenge, it's easy to get lost in complexity, exploring every possible angle or overengineering a solution. But some of the most effective solutions are also the simplest. A Sales Engineer who approaches a problem with simplicity in mind prioritizes clarity and practicality over sophistication for its own sake. This mindset not only leads to faster resolutions but also ensures that solutions are easier to implement, maintain, and scale.

The art of simplicity extends to the design of technical demonstrations. A cluttered demo that attempts to showcase every feature risks overwhelming the audience and diluting the message. A focused demo, on the other hand, highlights the most relevant capabilities, tying them directly to the client's goals. This approach requires discipline and foresight, the discipline to pare down to the essentials and the foresight to anticipate what will resonate most with the audience. Simplicity in demos doesn't just make them more effective; it elevates them to a level of elegance that reflects true mastery.

One of the barriers to simplicity is fear. There is often a concern that simplifying will make a solution seem less impressive or that it won't fully capture the depth of its capabilities. But simplicity is not about dumbing down; it's about smartly narrowing focus. It's about saying, "I understand your problem so well that I can show you exactly what matters." This confidence, paired with clarity, builds trust and reinforces your expertise.

Simplicity also fosters efficiency, both for the Sales Engineer and the client. A streamlined solution is easier to explain, easier to understand, and easier to deploy. It reduces the cognitive load on everyone involved, creating a smoother path to success. For the client, simplicity often translates to faster implementation, lower costs, and greater satisfaction. For the Sales Engineer, it means fewer points of failure, clearer communication, and stronger alignment with the client's needs.

Developing an elegant style of solutioning takes practice. It requires a deep understanding of both the technical details and the client's perspective. It also requires the ability to prioritize, to discern what is most important and let go of the rest. This process is iterative, honed over time through experience, feedback, and reflection. Each engagement offers an opportunity to refine your approach, to strip away the unnecessary and focus on what truly matters.

Excellence through simplicity is not about taking shortcuts or cutting corners. It's about doing the hard work of distillation, of getting to the heart of the matter without losing its essence. It's about presenting solutions that are not only effective but also clear, relatable, and elegant. It's about recognizing that in a world overflowing with complexity, simplicity stands out.

In the end, simplicity is a hallmark of mastery. It reflects a level of understanding that goes beyond surface knowledge, a confidence that doesn't need to prove itself through excess. Sales Engineers who embrace simplicity elevate their craft, delivering solutions that resonate deeply and endure. Because simplicity isn't just about making things easier; it's about making them better.

Chapter 10: Becoming the Calm Within the Chaos

The world of Sales Engineering is one of constant motion, last-minute changes to proposals, technical challenges during demos, and the high-stakes tension of securing multi-million-dollar deals. In this swirling chaos, clients and colleagues alike look for something steady, a calm center to anchor their confidence. Becoming that calm within the chaos isn't just a valuable skill; it's the essence of leadership in the role of a Sales Engineer.

The ability to remain composed under pressure is not about suppressing stress or pretending that challenges don't exist. It's about cultivating a mindset of focus and resilience that allows you to navigate uncertainty with clarity. Stoicism provides a powerful framework for this. The philosophy emphasizes control over one's inner state,

regardless of external circumstances. Marcus Aurelius, a leader who governed during times of immense turmoil, once wrote, "You have power over your mind, not outside events. Realize this, and you will find strength." Sales Engineers can draw on this principle to build a steady foundation, becoming a source of calm even in the most turbulent scenarios.

When facing high-pressure situations, preparation becomes your first defense against chaos. Chaos often magnifies when you're unprepared, and preparation is your armor against the unexpected. This doesn't mean anticipating every possible scenario but equipping yourself with the tools and knowledge to adapt. For example, before a critical demo, a well-prepared Sales Engineer will have tested the system in multiple configurations, identified potential failure points, and rehearsed responses to likely questions. They'll also have a backup plan, and maybe even a backup for the backup. This thoroughness provides a safety net, allowing you to focus on execution rather than worrying about what might go wrong.

In the moment, mindfulness becomes the anchor that steadies the ship. Chaos often stems from an inability to stay present, as the mind races ahead to worst-case scenarios or replays past mistakes.

Mindfulness brings you back to the current moment, grounding you in what you can do right now. Techniques like deep breathing, brief meditative pauses, or simply focusing on your immediate surroundings can help you reset during moments of high tension. A Sales Engineer who takes a deep breath before answering a difficult question during a pitch communicates calm confidence, putting both themselves and their audience at ease.

Remaining calm doesn't just benefit you; it directly impacts how others perceive and trust you. Clients and internal teams alike are drawn to those who exude steadiness during uncertainty. When a Sales Engineer maintains composure in a crisis, it sends a message: "I can handle this, and so can you." This trust becomes a competitive advantage, especially in scenarios where the stakes are high and tensions are running hot.

You are the Sales Engineer leading a critical proposal review with a client's executive team. Midway through, a key stakeholder raises an unexpected objection, derailing the flow of the presentation. A reactive response might escalate the tension, but a calm and measured approach, acknowledging the concern, addressing it thoughtfully, and smoothly steering back on track, not only resolves the immediate issue but also strengthens the client's confidence in your abilities.

This calm center isn't just a tool for immediate challenges; it's a form of leadership. Leadership isn't reserved for those with formal titles; it's an approach to guiding others through challenges. In Sales Engineering, this often means being the person who remains unfazed when things don't go as planned. Stoicism teaches that while you can't control external events, you can always control your response. This mindset of responsibility and steadiness creates a ripple effect, calming the entire team and inspiring confidence. It ensures that you're a reliable partner, someone who can navigate competing demands without adding to the chaos. This doesn't mean suppressing emotion or avoiding difficult conversations; it means approaching challenges with a clear head and a focus on solutions.

Focus is the antidote to chaos, and developing it requires intentional practice. One effective method is prioritization. Not all fires are worth putting out immediately; some can burn a little longer without causing harm. A Sales Engineer must discern what demands immediate attention and what can wait, ensuring that energy is spent where it will have the greatest impact. This clarity not only improves efficiency but also prevents the overwhelm that leads to reactive decision-making. Chaos often feels overwhelming because it's easy to lose sight of the bigger picture. A setback in a single presentation or a delay in a project doesn't define the success of your career or even the engagement. By keeping long-term goals in mind, you can approach immediate challenges with a calm resolve, knowing that they are part of a larger journey.

Calmness is contagious. When you embody steadiness, it influences those around you, creating an environment where challenges are met with collaboration rather than conflict. Clients feel reassured, colleagues feel supported, and teams function more cohesively. This ripple effect amplifies your impact, extending your steadiness to every aspect of the engagement. It's not about eliminating challenges but mastering how you respond to them. It's about preparation, mindfulness, focus, and leadership through steadiness. In the ever-changing landscape of Sales Engineering, where complexity and high stakes are the norm, this ability isn't just a skill, it's a superpower. By cultivating calm, you don't just navigate chaos; you transform it into an opportunity to lead, inspire, and excel.

Chapter 11: The Endurance to Succeed

Success in Sales Engineering is not achieved in sprints. It is a marathon, an endurance test that challenges your focus, resilience, and adaptability over the long haul. The demands of the role are constant: evolving technologies, shifting client needs, and unrelenting pressure to deliver results. To succeed, you must cultivate the mindset of a long-distance runner, embracing long-term thinking and pacing yourself for the journey ahead. This endurance is not just about survival; it's about thriving, consistently delivering value, and building a career that stands the test of time.

Longevity in Sales Engineering begins with perspective. In the rush to meet quotas, close deals, and address immediate challenges, it's easy to lose sight of the bigger picture. But success is rarely defined by a single victory. It is the cumulative impact of consistent effort, thoughtful decisions, and meaningful relationships. Endurance requires you to look beyond the moment, to see your work not as a series of isolated tasks but as a continuous journey of growth and contribution. Each client interaction, every demo, and even the setbacks become part of a larger narrative, one that shapes not only your career but also your influence within the industry.

Embracing long-term thinking transforms the way you approach challenges. Consider the difference between reacting to a problem and responding with a long-term mindset. A Sales Engineer faced with a demanding client might be tempted to overpromise to secure a deal. In the short term, this approach might seem effective, but it often leads to complications down the line, strained relationships, unmet expectations, and diminished credibility. Long-term thinking, however, prioritizes trust and transparency. It recognizes that enduring success comes from building relationships rooted in honesty and delivering solutions that truly meet the client's needs. This mindset not only fosters loyalty but also positions you as a trusted advisor whose value extends far beyond individual engagements.

Stoicism offers profound insights into cultivating endurance. The philosophy teaches that true strength lies in focusing on what you can control, accepting what you cannot, and persevering with purpose. This perspective is invaluable in Sales Engineering, where uncertainty is a constant companion. You cannot control a client's budget cuts, a competitor's aggressive pricing, or a sudden shift in market conditions. But you can control your preparation, your adaptability, and your commitment to excellence. By focusing on these controllables, you build a foundation of resilience that enables you to endure challenges without losing momentum.

Endurance is also about embracing the iterative nature of growth. Every setback, every rejected proposal, and every challenging interaction is an opportunity to refine your skills and deepen your understanding. This iterative process mirrors the stoic belief that obstacles are not barriers but stepping stones. Each challenge you face adds to your experience, sharpening your expertise and strengthening your resolve. Over time, this accumulation of lessons transforms you from a competent practitioner into a masterful Sales Engineer.

Building a career of endurance also requires pacing yourself. The high-pressure environment of Sales Engineering can lead to burnout if not managed carefully. Endurance means recognizing that rest is not a weakness but a necessity. Just as a marathon runner must balance effort with recovery, you must prioritize self-care to sustain your performance. This includes not only physical well-being but also mental and emotional health. Practices like mindfulness, regular exercise, and setting boundaries around work can help you maintain the energy and focus needed to excel over the long term.

Longevity in Sales Engineering is deeply tied to the relationships you build. Clients, colleagues, and mentors all play a role in your journey. By cultivating relationships based on trust, respect, and mutual support, you create a network that sustains you through challenges and amplifies your successes. These relationships are not transactional; they are investments in a shared future. A client who trusts you becomes a repeat customer. A colleague who respects you becomes a collaborator. A mentor who believes in you becomes a source of guidance and inspiration. These connections form the foundation of a career that is not only enduring but also fulfilling.

The mindset of endurance also involves a willingness to adapt. The landscape of technology and business is constantly evolving, and what worked yesterday may not work tomorrow. Enduring Sales Engineers embrace this reality, staying curious, continuously learning, and remaining open to change. Adaptability ensures that you stay relevant and effective, no matter how the environment shifts. It transforms challenges into opportunities and positions you as a leader who thrives in uncertainty.

As you build a career of endurance, you also build a legacy. The impact of your work extends beyond individual deals and projects. It influences the clients you serve, the teams you collaborate with, and the industry you help shape. This legacy is not about accolades or recognition; it is about the difference you make and the values you embody. It is about being remembered not just for what you achieved but for how you approached your work, with integrity, dedication, and resilience.

Stoic principles offer a powerful framework for this journey. They teach that true fulfillment comes not from external rewards but from living in alignment with your values and striving for excellence in all that you do. This perspective transforms not only your career but also your life. It reminds you that success is not a destination but a process, one that requires patience, perseverance, and purpose.

Success in Sales Engineering is a marathon, not a sprint. It is a journey of continuous growth, guided by long-term thinking and sustained by resilience. It is about building relationships that last, adapting to change with grace, and finding fulfillment in the process. By embracing the endurance to succeed, you not only achieve your goals but also create a career that is meaningful, impactful, and enduring.

Chapter 12: The Legacy of a Sales Engineer

The legacy of a Sales Engineer is not written in quotas or deal sizes but in the relationships built, the trust earned, and the impact made. Success in this role transcends numbers on a spreadsheet. It's about leaving a lasting imprint, on clients, colleagues, and the industry as a whole. A legacy rooted in integrity and influence endures far longer than any quarterly target ever could.

Redefining success starts with rejecting the narrow definition that ties worth to immediate outcomes. In a competitive industry, it's tempting to equate success with closed deals or promotions. But true legacy lies in the ripple effects of your actions: the client who credits their success to your guidance, the junior colleague who learned resilience by watching your example, or the product team whose solutions were sharpened through your insights. Each interaction becomes a thread in the fabric of your career, contributing to a narrative of meaningful influence and impact.

Integrity is the cornerstone of this legacy. The Sales Engineer who prioritizes honesty over convenience, who is transparent about limitations while championing strengths, creates a reputation that resonates deeply. Clients may not remember every detail of your proposal, but they will remember how you made them feel, whether they trusted you, whether you respected their time and challenges, and whether you approached your work with authenticity. Integrity is not just an ethical choice; it's a strategic one. It builds the kind of trust that transforms one-off transactions into lasting partnerships and fleeting interactions into enduring relationships.

The stoic approach to legacy offers profound lessons for Sales Engineers. Stoicism teaches that external recognition is fleeting, while the values we embody define us. Marcus Aurelius advised, "Waste no more time arguing about what a good man should be. Be one." In Sales Engineering, this translates to focusing on what truly matters, solving problems, creating value, and acting with purpose. A stoic mindset anchors you in the present, reminding you that legacy is built not in grand gestures but in the quiet consistency of your actions.

Consider the Sales Engineer who faces a high-stakes decision: push a product feature that doesn't quite align with the client's needs to close a deal, or advocate for a more suitable but less lucrative alternative. The stoic approach chooses the latter. It values long-term impact over short-term gain. The client may not immediately see the integrity behind this choice, but over time, they'll recognize you as a partner who puts their interests first. That's how legacies are built, one principled decision at a time.

Building a lasting reputation also means embracing collaboration over competition. Sales Engineering is rarely a solo endeavor. It thrives on teamwork, shared knowledge, and collective success. The Sales Engineer who lifts others up, who mentors, who listens, who shares credit, leaves a legacy not just of individual achievement but of community and connection. This collaborative spirit creates a ripple effect, inspiring others to adopt the same approach and amplifying your influence far beyond your immediate reach.

The impact of a Sales Engineer's legacy extends beyond the professional sphere. The principles and values you cultivate in your work often influence the way you navigate life. Integrity, resilience, and the ability to focus on what truly matters are not confined to client meetings or technical demos; they shape your interactions with family, friends, and the broader world. A life lived with purpose and alignment is itself a legacy, one that inspires and uplifts those around you.

Breaking the fear bubbles that hold you back is an essential part of this journey. Fear is often the greatest obstacle to creating a meaningful legacy. Fear of rejection, fear of failure, or fear of stepping outside your comfort zone can keep you anchored in mediocrity. But every time you confront those fears, every time you choose courage over caution, you expand your capacity for impact. Breaking the fear bubble is not just about personal growth; it's about setting an example for others. It shows your colleagues, your clients, and your peers what's possible when fear is replaced with action and doubt with determination. It is this courage, repeated and shared, that transforms the role of Sales Engineer into one of profound influence.

As this book comes to a close, the call to action is clear: redefine what it means to be a Sales Engineer. Step beyond the confines of quotas and technical mastery. Embrace the deeper aspects of the role, the relationships, the integrity, the influence. Adopt a stoic mindset that values process over outcomes, long-term impact over immediate gains, and purpose over prestige. By doing so, you don't just succeed; you transform the role of Sales Engineer into something greater. You leave a legacy that matters.

A legacy is not built in a day or even in a year. It's the accumulation of countless moments, the conversations, the decisions, the actions that define your career and your character. It's the trust you build, the problems you solve, and the lives you touch. And it's the example you set, proving that Sales Engineering is not just about selling solutions; it's about creating value, fostering connections, and making a difference. That is the legacy of a Sales Engineer. It is a legacy that transcends individual success, leaving a mark on the industry and inspiring those who follow to aim higher, think deeper, and work with greater purpose.

Chris Fontaine

The Fear Bubble: A Sales Engineer's Call to Action

As we close this journey together, it's time to reflect, not on the challenges that Sales Engineers face, nor the obstacles that sometimes cloud our path, but on the enduring nature of the fear bubble and what it represents. The fear bubble isn't something we pop and leave behind forever. It's persistent, always waiting at the edges of our growth, ready to reappear when stakes rise or uncertainty looms. But this is its purpose: to remind us that fear isn't an endpoint but an ever-present companion to progress.

The role of a Sales Engineer is one of immense responsibility and complexity. You are translators of possibility, bridging the gap between technical innovation and human understanding. It is a role that demands clarity in the face of ambiguity, confidence in the presence of doubt, and, most importantly, the courage to step into discomfort repeatedly. The fear bubble may never be gone, but its presence is no longer a barrier; it becomes a signal of where we are meant to grow.

Throughout this book, we've explored principles that aren't just concepts but tools for transforming the way you approach your work. Stoicism teaches us to embrace what we can control and accept what we cannot, to see obstacles not as deterrents but as pathways. Each rejection, setback, and challenge is an opportunity, not to eliminate fear but to act in spite of it. This is the core of breaking the fear bubble: it's not a single moment of triumph but a series of choices to engage with fear rather than retreat from it.

Legacy is built in these choices. It is not defined by quotas or accolades but by the relationships you nurture, the trust you cultivate, and the solutions you create that resonate long after the work is done. The Sales Engineer who listens deeply to a client's concerns, who collaborates with humility, and who delivers clarity where there was once confusion leaves a mark far greater than any single deal. Your legacy is written not in moments of glory but in the consistency of your actions, the quiet, steady decisions that demonstrate integrity, resilience, and purpose.

Consider the role of integrity in this journey. A Sales Engineer who values long-term trust over short-term wins creates a reputation that endures. Whether it's being honest about a product's limitations or advocating for what truly serves the client, these moments define how you are remembered. Clients may not recall every feature or detail of your solution, but they will remember how you approached them, whether you prioritized their needs, respected their challenges, and showed up with authenticity. Integrity doesn't just earn trust; it cements your role as a partner, not just a vendor.

Collaboration, too, is essential to your legacy. Sales Engineering is rarely a solo endeavor. The best outcomes are born from teamwork, from listening to colleagues, sharing credit, and uplifting those around you. Collaboration without ego creates ripple effects. It fosters environments where innovation thrives, where clients feel supported, and where colleagues feel inspired. The Sales Engineer who collaborates with humility builds not just solutions but communities of trust and respect.

The enduring presence of the fear bubble challenges us to redefine success. Success isn't about erasing fear; it's about moving forward despite it. It's about transforming fear into a catalyst for action, a signal of importance. Every time you step into discomfort, whether it's presenting to a skeptical audience or navigating the uncertainty of a new solution, you expand your capacity to lead and to make an impact. Fear is not the enemy; it is the guidepost pointing you toward growth.

As this book comes to a close, the call to action is clear. Sales Engineers have the unique ability to bridge the gap between the technical and the human, to create solutions that matter, and to inspire trust in an uncertain world. This isn't just a role; it's a responsibility. Step forward with purpose. Break the fear bubble not by eliminating it but by facing it, time and again, with courage and clarity.

Redefine what it means to be a Sales Engineer. Go beyond quotas and technical mastery. Be the trusted partner, the collaborative leader, and the resilient innovator. Build a legacy not of fleeting wins but of lasting impact, one that inspires others to aim higher, think deeper, and act with integrity. Because at the end of the day, the fear bubble is not something to conquer once and for all. It is something to confront, embrace, and transform, over and over again. And in doing so, you don't just succeed, you lead.

The future of Sales Engineering is fearless, not because fear disappears, but because we learn to thrive alongside it. That is your challenge, your opportunity, and your legacy. The world is waiting for leaders who don't just navigate fear but use it as a springboard for greatness. Go forth and be the Sales Engineer who changes the game. The best is yet to come.

www.ingramcontent.com/pod-product-compliance
Lightning Source LLC
Chambersburg PA
CBHW071037240526
45469CB00006BD/2242